SO YOU ARE IN CHARGE

THINGS YOU SHOULD KNOW
IF YOU WANT TO STAY THERE

ALLEN M. DAUGHERTY

BALBOA.PRESS
A DIVISION OF HAY HOUSE

Balboa Press books may be ordered through booksellers or by contacting:

Balboa Press
A Division of Hay House
1663 Liberty Drive
Bloomington, IN 47403
www.balboapress.com
844-682-1282

Print information available on the last page.

ISBN: 978-1-9822-6277-8 (sc)
ISBN: 978-1-9822-6278-5 (e)

Balboa Press rev. date: 01/25/2021

PREFACE

I would like to say some things right off the bat about this book. First of all, every manager and leader should have a habit of reading good books on management and leadership. There are so many good books out there that can really help you be your best and succeed in your role. Some of these books really go deep into learning styles, personality traits, and proven management skills. I have read tons of them and attribute any success I have had in leadership to them. Basically, I am saying that if you don't take time to read and learn, operating on what you know won't help you raise the bar.

All my books are very informal and written in a conversational manner. I want to talk to you as if we were sitting together. I use simple facts and illustrations. I call it my 'peanut butter and jelly' approach. Very easy to digest. I will not be delving into psychological or philosophical concepts, just simple down to earth nuggets that I hope will be helpful. I won't be using a ton of big words mostly because I really don't know many. I will use humor at times because, well because I am just a funny guy and humor helps break things up a bit. It is not going to be advice from a highly educated, expert leader but just a few things I have seen from the 'Cheap Seats' as a little guy.

Leadership has always just seemed to fall into my hands. I joined the USAF at seventeen and a half. In tech school at Sheppard AFB in Texas, I was eventually promoted to a Red Rope, which meant I was in charge of marching an entire squadron around. Air Force folks may remember those good old days.

I did a tour in Spain, then returned to the states. During my second assignment, I worked in a pediatric clinic. When the manager, Non-Commissioned Officer in Charge, (NCOIC) left, I was promoted into that role. There were others that had been in longer, but they gave the job to me.

A few years later, I went to an independent duty site in England. When the NCOIC there was transferred, guess what? Yep, they put me in that role. I got out of the service and eventually became a dialysis technician, and in 1999, became a Registered Nurse. I took a job offer in Virginia, to be a floor nurse. I was only there for a week when the manager resigned and guess who they asked to take over? Right again, boy you are good at this guessing thing.

I ran that clinic for four years and then the Director of Operations resigned. I am not even going to tell you but yep, you are right. I am not bragging at all, but I wanted to give you a little idea of my experience and bring up a vital subject that we will look at in more detail in just a bit. Leadership comes naturally to some people and others recognize it.

Let's dive right in and I hope you will enjoy the book. There may be some things that you disagree with and that's perfectly okay. You have probably been wrong in the past as well (HAHA, I mean LOL). Here we go!

CONTENTS

CHAPTER 1

MANAGING

As we begin, let's just establish as a reference point that you are a manager in a medium sized restaurant. Not sure why I picked a restaurant, I'll try not to make us all hungry. You oversee greeters, the wait staff, cooks, dishwashers, a couple administrative folks, and the custodial crew. So, just what does it mean to be the manager? What are you managing? Here is a very simple definition of managing that helps me keep things in perspective.

Managing is, **'Exercising oversight to ensure satisfactory completion of pre-determined goals.'** Management is an exceptionally large umbrella that covers many sub-roles. Managers must manage people, processes, physical plant needs, and the ensuing results. A few things you must manage in this restaurant include the staff, the supply and food ordering, equipment maintenance, customer service, quality, finances, promotion and so much more.

Let us start by talking about managing people for a just a minute here as we will be diving deeper into the subject in other chapters. First, three important questions.

1. **Does the manager have to know how to do all the things that the staff are hired to do?** You say, 'Well how does someone manage cooks if they do not know how to cook?' That is a good question. The manager

1

is not managing the cooking, he is managing the cooks. If there is something wrong with the quality of the cooking, the manager manages the cooks by holding them accountable to the satisfactory completion of their goals. The manager wouldn't ask, 'Did you put too much garlic in?' They would ask, 'What recipe are you following to prepare that dish?' Think about it for a minute. Do CEOs in hospitals know how to do everything that the entire hospital staff does? Can they do open heart surgery, or lower the rate on an IV pump? No, they manage the entire gamut of operations in the hospital, but they can't perform every task.

2. **Is the manager responsible for all the teaching and training required for the various roles?** Watch the terms! *Responsible for, yes; doing it all, no.* The manager needs to ensure that the training program will meet the needs of the employee and prepare them to succeed. The training can be broken down into two main categories. One is role specific which I call technical; the ins and outs of what they were hired to do. The other category is the general things such as cleanliness, attire, clocking in and out, lunch and breaks, basic orientation, and etc. Managers here usually develop a thorough checklist to ensure nothing gets missed. Make sure you have good people doing your training so that your new people are not set up to fail. That brings us to the last question and the great perplexity in management:

3. **Is the manager responsible for everything under his supervision? The answer is YES.** Here is where the management skills that you learned from all those other books I was talking about come in. QUESTION: How can I handle the cook situation without knowing how to cook? If it is something that you can identify as a problem, then you can help. For example, what if the complaint is that the food is cool when it gets to the customer? Perhaps, you observe the cook leaving things on the counter too long after they are prepared. A little conversation on the problem can rectify it immediately. If the problem is overly bland chili, without knowing how to prepare chili, the manager is a bit out of his league. Here is where a good manager uses what I call, Subject Matter Experts (SME) to help him identify and correct problems. The SME here may be a more experienced cook that always gets good reviews on his cooking or perhaps can appoint a lead chef. Now, I know you; you have a lead chef, lead waitress, and a cleaning supervisor. Great job there, manager.

To summarize what we have discussed above, you do not know how to do everything those on your team do, thus, you cannot train them in the technical aspects of their roles, YET you are responsible for managing the end result. I guess I would have to classify management as one of the hardest occupations one can get into. However, successful managers will tell you that it is also one of the most rewarding.

People in charge are often given other unstated roles that are more descriptive of the actions they manage. Sometimes referred to as a Coach, the manager actively participates in helping their employees develop certain skillsets that can be beneficial to them.

SENARIO:

Lilly is a good waitress but pulls in the lowest tip total and seldom gets a good review. Watch this interaction.

"Lilly, may I talk to you for a minute?"

"Sure."

"Lilly, you are a good waitress and please don't get upset, everything is okay, and no one has complained, but I wonder if you would be open to a little coaching?"

"Yes Mike, I would."

"You take orders, deliver food, and really take good care of your customers. I would say that you do that as well as the others, but they are all making much more in tips than you are, and you seldom get any reviews from the customers. Again, you are not in trouble, but I was wondering what you thought about that?"

"I don't know. I just don't have a real bubbly personality and don't socialize much, I guess. The others do and I know the customers love that."

"Okay, great observation. I want to try something... smile."

"Smile?"

"Yes, I want to see you smile." And so, Lilly smiled. "Wow,

what a nice smile. I hardly ever see that. Now, look me in the eyes." As she did, she actually started laughing.

"You are nuts."

"I have heard that before, but I am just trying to help here. Let's try something. For the rest of the week, I want you to consciously smile while interacting with the customers and look them directly in the eye when they are looking at you. Let's start there and we will meet again to see how it went."

Mike doesn't know much about table waiting, but he does know a lot about people and knows the value of smiling and direct eye contact in customer service. He acted her as a coach. Lilly, by the way, received $5,000 in tips by the end of the week, quit waitressing and opened her own charm school (I may be exaggerating just a bit).

Managers are also mentors in many ways. We will discuss this in more detail in another chapter, but mentoring involves being a trusted guide and advisor. This role may or may not deal directly with work performance. Most of the time, it has to do with helping the employees reach their full potential and progress toward the accomplishment of their goals. Employees are human beings that have troubles, hard times, hurts, losses and occasionally need a guiding hand.

Managers are often needed to take off that supervisor hat, be a confidant and help with pressing issues. Sometimes, it can be in the form of a little career guidance as you not only have additional knowledge but experience as well.

I was in management for over 25 years and I can't count how many employees I mentored, leading to their career advancement. Again, no bragging here, just saying as a manager, you will have an opportunity to mentor those that work for you and that yields great rewards.

I have been blessed with being able to mentor so many employees that started out in an entry level position and are now in mid to upper-level management. When I see an email from them, as I sometimes do, and see their titles, I have to smile. That is true fulfillment.

By the way, not everyone wants to go into management, and we will discuss that later in more detail. Many may just want to progress in the roles that they are in and perhaps, further their education.

Sometimes, mentoring crosses over into the personal realm. In those cases, I have always avoided making recommendations but rather just LISTENED and posed a few questions that help them think in a broader way. People often have financial problems, (NOTE: You are a mentor not a loaning institution) family problems, and even some psychological problems, such as depression. These are not good areas to give advice on. You can listen, ask some questions to help them have clarity, and point them to others that can offer professional assistance. Please take this paragraph seriously as it can save you and them a world of trouble.

Good managers will recognize the need to transform themselves into good leaders. There has been much written about the difference between leadership and management. Just hearing both words provides insight to their difference. When you hear 'manage', you lean toward that person who is results driven, looking at performance. The word 'leader', on the other hand, infers a more personal approach to oversight. I have often said that managers manage things where leaders lead people. That is not really accurate but does show where the emphasis is.

No matter how technologically advanced we get, the most valuable asset that any supervisor has is their team. It would only make sense that a great deal of emphasis in supervision should be on leading them to achieve the set goals. Let me share a few statements that may help differentiate the two.

1. The manager looks at the end of the day to see how productive it was; the leader inspires and motivates his team during the day to achieve and exceed.
2. The manager is always looking for ways to improve quality and performance; the leader is always looking for ways to develop each employee to their top potential.
3. The manager says, 'I would like to share with you my goals for the upcoming year'; the leader says, 'Let's talk about some goals that WE can set for the upcoming year'.
4. The manager starts meetings off by saying, 'Okay, I have identified a few areas that we can focus on to improve.' The leader starts out, 'As we start this meeting, I want to recognize some of the team for their tremendous efforts and contributions.'
5. The manager uses the same *universal*, rah, rah, speech when it's time for motivating the team; the leader

takes time to learn what motivates each *individual* and does so accordingly.

6. The manager usually focuses on the present condition and short-term goals; the manager looks toward the future and on the long-term goals.

7. The manager is big at sharing the 'what and how'; the leader ensures they understand the 'why.'

Obviously, we could go on and on, but I think you get the idea and probably know several more differences that I did not mention. Most supervisors are a combination of the two but are weighted more on one side than the other. If you are a supervisor, pause for a minute and ask yourself, 'Am I more like a manager or am I more like a leader?'

CHAPTER 2

WHY MANAGEMENT?

The big question I want to ask here is, 'What made you want to become a manager or why do you want to become a manager?' I can't even estimate how many people I have interviewed for jobs in the nursing field. One question that I always asked was, 'Tell me a little about WHY you got into the medical field.' When you are caring for patients, the 'why' is very important.

The same goes for management positions. Why you want a role in management is extremely important, not only to those that are hiring, but also to you. I have had scores of managers working for me over the years; some are still in their management roles; some are out if it, doing something else that they felt was a better fit for their lifestyle; and some didn't last 18 months in their management role. The key, again, is the 'why'. Let me make just a few statements here on this subject; your 'why'.

1. If it's just for the money, do yourself a big favor, find another way to make more money. Taking on a management role with money as your main motivation is probably the top reason why managers don't last. EXAMPLE: A Nurse is making $25 an hour. She takes a promotion into management and gets paid $30 an hour. She is salaried now and

generally works 50 hours a week. That computes to $25.60 an hour (No overtime for salaried people). Sixty cents an hour is not worth a jump into management.

2. If it's just to get a title and an office and some business cards, (I am chuckling as I write this, but I am gonna be blunt) GET OVER IT. There is more to life than just attaining a title or status. I know so many nurses and technicians that have been doing what they have been doing for over 20 years, never venturing into management. They love what they do, they are good at what they do, and they are happy as can be, possessing great satisfaction and fulfillment in their jobs. By the way, most of them are true leaders on their teams, they just haven't stepped into any management positions.

3. If it's because you are great at what you do and everyone thinks you would be a good manager, please reevaluate. This happens so many times. Just because someone is great at what they do, does not mean that they will be good at management. Companies are notorious for taking a great worker, out of their role, place them into management, only for them to fail. Now, some people who are great at their jobs can indeed be great managers as well, but they better have some leadership traits and not just be good at their job. I spent 12 years in the USAF and loved it. In the military however, the longer you are in, usually the higher the rank you attain and the higher your

rank, the higher level of management you are in. Basically, if you have been in 20 years, you would probably be in charge of a large organization and you may not have one lick of leadership ability. They hold leadership training continuously throughout your career, but the truth is—you can teach someone all about leadership, but you still can't make someone a good leader.

4. If it is because you want to make a difference, feel like you were made to be a leader, enjoy teaching, mentoring, managing, coaching and really care about people; well, that's much better. Remember this point when you get to #2 below.

I want to share something that I think will illustrate a point. When I first got hired into dialysis, I was a Patient Care Technician (PCT). Sometimes, there were a few of us together on break or at lunch together. Oftentimes, the conversation sounded like this.

"Boy, I wish I was one of the nurses. They have no idea how hard we work, and they seem to sit an awful lot."

"Ya, just do assessments, give meds, and play on the computer."

"Ya, what a job."

Then, I went to nursing school and became a nurse. Sitting in the break room with other nurses, the conversation was like this.

"Boy, I wish I were the manager. Sitting in the office all day while we bust our butts."

"Ya, she pops out once and a while and looks busy then back into her office."

"Man, what a job."

Then, I became a manager. In a meeting with other managers, we would talk a bit as we waited for the Director. The conversation went like this:

"I sure wish I had her job. Just travel all over the place, everyone gets nervous when she walks into the clinics, goes to meetings all over the country."

"While we bust our butts managing the clinics and she gets the big bucks."

Then, I became a Director. When we gathered for... Haha. I'll spare you the details. I think you see what I am talking about. So, a few statements about the 'WHY'.

1. When you are thinking about the 'what' (what you will be doing) at that next level, **there is always more to it than you think**. It is never as easy as it looks. For example, the team on the floor sees the manager spending a lot of time in their office. They equate that with not working hard because it is not involving physical labor. But, there is (here is your chance to cheer managers) making the schedule and trying to please everyone, for starters; doing payroll, checking over the finances, taking numerous phone calls and being on several conference calls, keeping up with employee personnel and education files, checking on quality performance, ensuring readiness for surveys and inspections—the list goes on!

2. **If you don't have a substantial 'why' for getting into management, the 'what' will be your Waterloo.** Sooner or later, managers realize how tough of a job management really is. It can become very stressful and the no-win scenarios seem to keep rolling in. Just as you say that was the straw that broke the camel's back, another bail comes along. As soon as you get one problem resolved, two more arise to take its place. I am not trying to paint a gloomy picture of management, but I am saying that if you do not have very solid reasons for wanting to be a manager, chances are, you will hang it up. I can't even count the number of resignations and phone calls I have gotten in the past saying, 'I just can't do this anymore'. What they are really saying is; 'The demands and stressfulness of the job now outweigh the reasons I had for taking it. The prestige, the office, the business cards, and the title are just not worth it. Those of you that are managers have probably gotten to that point several times. The difference is that you were in it for the right reasons and you stayed.

I have got to share this experience with you because it depicts what I am trying to say. I told you about my first dialysis management position. I had moved to Virginia to take a staff nursing role and a few days after I arrived the manager resigned. I was really looking forward to helping her because I could see so many things that needed to be fixed and she just seemed so stressed and overwhelmed.

The Director called me into the office and told me that the manager had resigned and asked me if I was interested in taking the role. I told her I would under one condition; that I could make the changes that I felt need to be made and that she would support them. She agreed with the caveat that we discussed the changes first, which was great by me. Before I go on to tell you about the second most difficult period in my life, I want to talk about my, 'why'.

When I started working in dialysis, I really fell in love with the patients. I loved taking care of them and getting to know them. I had found my occupational niche. I really cared about them and if I helped them in any way, my day was complete.

When I saw the patients in this clinic, I knew things needed to change in order for them to get the best possible care. I could do some good as the nurse, but I could affect the entire clinic as the manager, that was my, 'why' and when hard times came, it got me through them. It got so bad that when I arrived at the clinic, I would sit in my truck and grasp the steering wheel and ask myself, 'Is it really worth it?' Then, I could see the faces of those precious patients and would go in to face another day. My, 'why' outweighed any obstacle that came my way.

To make a long, nightmarish story short, a year later, the only one left from the original team was my secretary. The necessary changes were made, and it became a top-notch clinic.

People in all walks of life can endure quite a bit when their 'why' is strong enough. If it isn't, it doesn't take much to get them to quit. I'm not saying that everyone that gets out of management does so because they didn't have the right motives for getting in. Many just need a change after serving as a manager for years and some have lifestyle changes where a different job may be a better fit. What I am saying is, before you get into management, ask yourself WHY?

CHAPTER 3

QUALITIES OF A MANAGER

Before we jump into what I consider to be the qualities every manager needs to have, I want to make a few general statements. First of all, as adults, qualities are traits found to be in someone, not things that can be taught and learned. Our character begins forming when we are young. Often, opposing characteristics are encountered, giving options as to how we will develop. Then, we go through a period of decision making as to the characteristics we want to incorporate into our lives. Those decisions create a pattern, and that pattern will produce a personality trait in that individual.

Ever heard anyone say, 'That Mary, she has *always* been so big hearted.' Or 'That Frank has been in trouble *all of his life*. Not an honest bone in his body.' In both cases, they were exposed early in life to certain traits, they were practiced for a period of time, and finally became a trait or quality of their personality. Thank goodness, the will of man can override childhood environmental influences and good can prevail. On the other hand, no matter how good that early environment is, sometimes, the opposite is true as well.

Secondly, I want to say that although you can't learn qualities, you can learn how valuable qualities are to your role and to your life and **begin to construct good qualities.** In a bit, we are going to be talking about managers having the quality of patience. I want to give you a personal illustration here to explain what I just said; **good qualities that you did not have can be constructed later on.** (Most of the time, when I use me as an example, it is of what NOT to do. Ouch!)

While I was growing up, my pants were on fire. I wanted to do it now. I wanted to go now. I had little time for waiting or later, it was always now. I had to get my driver's license the first day I was eligible. I signed up for the USAF at seventeen and a half years old and left home six days after I graduated High School. My mother used to say that I never sat long enough to get one wrinkle on the seat of my pants.

Then, I got married. Sorry, I am laughing because I can see the smiles on all your faces as you think of your spouse.

"Hey, honey, let's run to the store real quick to pick up a few things."

"Okay, I'll be ready in a minute."

Now, why don't they just say up front, "I'll be ready in about 45 minutes?" First of all, a minute is a minute and to an inpatient person, anything over that is torture. Secondly, I didn't say, "Let's go SOMETIME today". I said "Real quick". Marriage will teach you how important patience is and even help you develop it, hopefully. (It's kind of a Pass / Fail test; you know, do or die.)

The children came, then a management position and abra kadabra, I am now a very patient person. So, you can learn how important it is, practice it diligently and then it can certainly become a trait in your personality. It is not easy, but it can be done. Let's look at a few important qualities of a leader.

Respect is a huge word in life and in management as well. There are many paths to respect, and we are going to look at how these qualities lead there. If you think about it, you can respect a person's position but not respect them as a person. For example, I have had a few supervisors where I had respect for their position as my supervisor, but I didn't respect them as a person because of some poor qualities they possessed.

I certainly respect those in government positions because of their positions, but that doesn't mean that I respect them as people. Position respect is implied by the nature of the position; personal respect is freely given because it is earned. I have had many supervisors that I gave my total respect to, not just because their title demanded respect, but because their personal traits earned it.

So, with that as a backdrop, let's look at:

Possess Honesty and Integrity

Okay, here is the chain. Someone says some things and they are proven to be true. I have a basis to believe them and so they have earned my trust; and trust is a pathway to respect. I could spend several pages on telling you how important it is for a manager to be honest. You need them to be able to trust you and if you are proven to be dishonest, that trust will never be there and so the respect that they may have for you will be tarnished. It's like walking out on an old wooden bridge. Three steps out and a plank breaks and you nearly fall through. How much farther are you going to go out on that bridge? You will stop right there, and so will the trust of individuals that someone has been dishonest with. It stops right there.

It is not hard to trust someone that has never been dishonest with you. It is really hard for someone that has been dishonest to gain that trust back.

Thinking back to our conversation on leadership, it is easy to see why a manager must have honesty and integrity. Leaders lead so that others can follow. Sometimes, a manager can push from behind, but leaders lead from the front. In order to be a leader and to have others follow, they need to be able to be trusted. So, in order to be trusted, they should always be truthful (honesty) and always do the right things (integrity).

Let's look at an illustration. John is someone you work with. He often comes in late and makes up stories to excuse his tardiness. You have seen him take things that belong to the company home. He lies to his wife about where he is going after work so he can go bet on the horses. One day, John comes to you with a 'wonderful' business proposal that is ground floor and all you need to do is pitch in $3,000. Is he an honest person; does he always tell the truth? No! Does he have integrity; does he always do the right thing? No. Do you trust him? Of course not—and you just saved $3,000.

Had John always been honest and showed that he was a man of integrity, you may have at least taken a look at it. Sometimes, following the daily routines don't require a lot of change. You can pretty much do what you always do. But, when new things come out and changes are made; basically, headed into uncharted waters, you need to be able to trust the leadership of the manager.

Have you ever been going on a familiar trip and come across a detour? You're cruising along, doing fine, almost on autopilot when you see that horrible sign; 'Road Closed Ahead; Take Detour'. Well, you get off the road, make a few turns here and there and soon you realize that you have no idea where you are. All you can do now is trust those Detour signs to get you back to your original route.

Here is a really important fact. When someone is in a new job, at a new place, and they don't know much about what is going on, it is extremely important that they are able to trust their manager. They are counting on their leadership for guidance and direction during those first few critical months.

I have sat in break rooms and heard staff members talking about how unreliable the manager was *in front of new employees*. Those staff members should not have been doing that. What they were saying may have been true but that is not information to be blurting out in a break room in front of new employees. However, managers need to have such a high degree of honesty and integrity that this would never happen and if it did, the new employees would soon find out that they were just false accusations from probably some disgruntled staff members.

Honesty and integrity build trust, and trust helps people follow the leader and respect them.

Fair and Impartial

This area is so vitally important, but it is also sometimes hard to discuss. Just a few statements before we dive in.

1. Everyone, without reservation, deserves to be treated fairly.
2. Some things may seem fair but when partiality is involved, can be described as unfair.
3. Many times, impartiality is due to professional relationships crossing that line into personal relationships.
4. Once a manager is seen as being impartial and thus unfair, they lose respect very quickly.

No one in this particular workplace enjoys working Saturdays. Nancy notices that she is scheduled to work every other Saturday, thus having every other Saturday off. It seems like a pretty fair schedule. Then, she notices that Barb, who happens to eat lunch with the manager every day and occasionally connects with the manager after work has every weekend off. This is perceived as partiality (and well could be) and thus now the schedule is unfair.

I have heard many managers say that not everyone needs to know why certain things are done or certain actions are taken. We have to remember that *perception is reality if there is no clarity*. Managers must make sure that they are as transparent as they can be to avoid misinterpreted actions and perceptions.

Let's run with this just a bit further. The reason Barb is off every weekend is because Bill needed a couple extra days off during the week, so he traded for his Saturdays off. If Nancy had checked previous schedules, she would have seen that Barb was also working every other Saturday. The manager could have provided a little extra clarity by explaining the trades on the schedule. Yes, that is going a bit far but again it is worth it to have the reputation of being fair and not showing partiality. You would not believe how many times over the years I have heard staff say that so and so was the manager's favorite and gets anything she wants. Managers cannot have favorites but must always be fair and impartial.

On the other hand, if the manager and Barb were talking and Barb expressed how much she hated working Saturdays and that was the reasoning for the change; there is a partiality issue there.

Let's keep Nancy and Barb around for another scenario. There has been a bit of a problem with tardiness. The manager makes a rule that from that point on, anyone late with have a verbal counselling session and it will be documented in their records. Nancy was one of the prime offenders and sure enough on Tuesday, she shows up late again with no valid explanation.

On the other hand, Barb has worked there several years and has never been late, until (yep, you guessed it) Tuesday. Her car wouldn't start, and she had to wait for someone to bring her to work. According to the newly established policy, who would get the verbal counselling session? Both correct? What does the manager really want to do? I think you know the answer there, but to be fair and impartial, she did the right thing.

Sometimes, it is hard as a manager not to get a little closer to some of the team than the others. You usually have more respect for and spend more time with the stellar performers. They are often given additional responsibilities and thus you need more face time with them. Just always make sure to spend quality time with everyone. That shows them that you do not have your, 'favorites', and remember, with time and additional training, the others can also become stellar employees. Managers have to build the WHOLE team.

Appreciative; Using Praise and Recognition

Seems like we have been looking at the negative aspect of things, so let's switch over to the positive. Praise and recognition are very important tools in motivating people. Some people say that they don't like it when they get praised or recognized; deep down, they do. Just a few points here:

1. You should always be looking for ways to thank, praise, and recognize people and their accomplishments. Anyone will tell you that when you make a mistake, you are very quick to hear about it. But, work your butt off and even go the extra mile and no one says anything. Managers have an opportunity to change that perception. It does have to be sincere and worthy of recognition though. "I want to recognize Steven for showing up for work all week without being late." I would leave that one go. If you do that, it makes

recognition look cheap and insincere. But "I want to thank Steven for his efforts yesterday. He was finished with his section early but stayed after to help a couple of others that were behind." Now, that's the ticket.

2. It is always good to give constructive feedback privately but give praise and recognition publicly. Recognition means that you identified something that they did worthy of mention and you announced it publicly so others would also know about it. Hey, they love a good praise from the boss in the office, but in front of others, watch that smile develop, and their chest stick out. I received several medals while in the Air Force. The Commander didn't call me over to his office and pin it on. He waited until the monthly awards banquet, with scores of people there. Boy was that exciting. Made me want to go out and earn another one and by the way, that's what it's all about.

3. Make sure everyone knows the common goals of the workplace and also other opportunities for additional accomplishments. Give them a way to work for and earn that recognition. Once, at a clinic, I was running over budget on supplies. At a meeting, I asked for input on how we could save money on supplies. A bunch of great ideas came in, and the contributors were recognized.

4. Sometimes, a simple "Thank you, I really appreciate that." will do. It may have been something little but

always show gratitude, even for the little things. By the way, notice the difference here. It may seem so miniscule, but it makes a huge difference when you say it.

"Thank you! I want you to know that I really appreciate that." vs

"Thank you! I want you to know that I really appreciate **YOU** and all you do for us." This shows that you appreciate them as a person as well as what they do.

Appreciation, praise, and recognition go a long way in developing the relationships you have with members of your team. Almost every management survey I have ever taken asks, "Do you feel that you are recognized for your accomplishments?" It really is a big deal so make sure you are mindful of the opportunities to deliver.

An Example

Like it or not, leaders are set up to be the example for the team to follow. Those of you that have been managers know that being an example all the time is not an easy task. I have heard this illustrated by comparing managers to the Master Clock, that everyone sets their time by. If you are correct, then they are as well. If you are off a bit, so will the entire team. It might not seem fair but that's the way it is with leadership.

I know what you are thinking. 'Managers are human, and they make mistakes too.' That is indeed true. However,

I didn't say that managers had to be PERFECT. I said they are the example. That means that if they do make mistakes, as we all do, they need to handle it in the appropriate manner. If you as a manager catch someone doing something wrong, you don't want to hear excuses, you don't want them to blame others, you just want, 'Hey, I messed up. I know what I did wrong and this is how I am going to keep that from happening again.' That is exactly how you should handle mistakes that you make.

At times, some managers work right alongside the others on the team doing the same work. In that instance, they should be following the policies and procedures in doing that job correctly. Say a manager in a welding shop is constantly reminding his team to wear goggles anytime they are actively welding. He walks out onto the floor and sees something that just needs a tiny touch up, so he grabs a torch and starts, no goggles. That is a really good example of what NOT to do.

If employees are expected to follow the rules, managers need to be good examples of the same. There are some general things where a manager can be a good example as well. Managers should always display good work ethics. They may not be doing the same thing, but should be working just as hard doing what they are doing. Coming in late, taking an hour and a half for lunch and going home early every day will not inspire maximum performance from the team.

Promptness is also important. If you promise that the schedule for the next month will be out by the 20th of the preceding month, make sure it is. If someone asks for something and you tell them that you will do it, don't put it off. The timeliness may not be important to you, but it could be to them. Now, we just have to jump into.

I was talking to a manger in a dialysis clinic once and she was telling me about how several of her staff members were complaining about the fact that she never came out to the floor to help them when they got busy. Our conversation went like this:

"They need to realize that I am the manager and I have lots of things to do here in my office."

I asked her if she was open for a little coaching and she said that she was.

"I want you to weigh these two scenarios. One, you go out to the floor and assist the team get over the hump. The staff sees that, and you are now their hero. They respect your willingness to help, knowing you do have other things that you need to do as well. When you do that, you do some bonding and deepen the relationships that you have with your staff. That, by the way, is priceless for a manager. Then you go back to your office and take care of the other things you had to do. You may have to work just a tad longer, but you get it done. As the staff leaves and sees you still working, they think, 'She took some time to help us and now she has to work a little later. That is some manager.'

The next day, the staff brought the manager some flowers, candy, coffee, a couple of books, a 60 in. widescreen TV and…ah, I think I got a little carried away. They did say thanks though.

"Or two, you can stay in your office and get your stuff done, miss out on the opportunity to bond with your team, and don't get to set a good example of teamwork. You have actually tarnished the relationships you have with your team and they lose a lot of respect for you. Now, which scenario is going to help you be a better manager and leader?"

I think you get the idea. She must not have because six months later she was no longer a manger.

Dependable

Let me start this section off by giving an example of what we are going to discuss. Jerry walked about 20 yards onto a rope bridge. He told his friend Bob that the bridge was strong and could hold both of them as they crossed.

"You believe me don't you, Bob?"

"Sure, I believe you. You would never lie to me about something like that."

"Come on out then."

Bob replied immediately, "Are you nuts? I don't have a death wish right now."

I don't know about you, but I am thinking that I would side with Bob. There are two things here that have to be dependable, the bridge and Jerry. It is obvious that Jerry counts the bridge as dependable because he is already out on it. Doubting Bob then either does not think that either Jerry or the bridge are dependable and thus doesn't move. Let's look at a few things about dependability and then we will come back to these guys. We don't want to leave Jerry out on that bridge while you finish reading the book.

1. Dependability is often earned through past performances. I have had many cars over the years that I would consider dependable. They started right up and got me to where I was going and back with no problems. I have had some others as well—starting up and breaking down were more of a tossup. They were not dependable. We want physicians, mechanics, financial advisors (and others) that are dependable to help us; and that is exactly what employees need in a manager. Work diligently to build the reputation of being dependable. Okay, remember Bob and Jerry? I want to tell you a secret. Jerry was there with some of his friends the weekend before and they all made it across the bridge. The bridge held up in past performances, Jerry knew it was dependable. (He never told Bob that and he is halfway back to the car.)

2. Dependability is not just saying you will but doing what you say you will do. Anyone can say, 'Hey, I got your back,' or 'I'm always there for you, or 'You can count on me.' When they see you come through for them, then they will know that you are dependable.

3. Being a dependable leader will inspire your team to go places where they have never gone before. I do a lot of traveling for work and as I do, I often have to rely on my GPS. Sometimes, if it is an easy to get to location, I look through the directions get there without the GPS. Going into large cities is another story. Getting lost in Atlanta one time before GPS was

a grueling experience. I wasn't afraid but aggravated because I keep driving and asking for directions and remained lost for at least an hour. (I did get to see a lot of the city though). Perhaps, you are bringing on a new line or starting a new procedure, doing things very differently. Your team is heading into uncharted territory so they will need to be able to depend on you to lead them through.

This trait is so important that I am surprised it isn't used in more business ads.

"This Handyman does it all." DependaBill

"This container keeps everything fresh." DependaBowl

"This toy will last for years." DependaBall

"It rings every time." DependaBell

"Improve the quality of your livestock." DependaBull

I know, leave the comedy to those that are actually funny. OK! I was going to mention something that elderly people occasionally have to wear but since I am getting old, I'll leave that one go. I think that shows how sensitive I am, but I guess that DEPENDS on how you look at it. Darn, I did it, didn't I?

Understanding

I am sure that there have been books written just on this one point. It is so vital that leaders are strong, have set goals, have standards, but also be understanding. Most of these examples have to do with people. We may have computers, machines, and fancy gadgets but the most valuable resource we have are the human beings that operate all of them and they require understanding. (I wish someone would have told my elementary and high school teachers that. I gave solid, good reasons why I didn't have my homework done, but they were just not…understanding).

Here is someone that wants to be a brain surgeon. Early in his schooling, he has to take Basic Anatomy and Physiology. He learns all the bones in the foot and all the blood vessels in the body and all the parts of the kidney and all the layers of the skin and…I could go on and on. But wait—he is studying to be a brain surgeon. Why on earth would he need to learn all of that? Because a thorough UNDERSTANDING of the body is necessary for him to become a good brain surgeon. And for managers to become good managers, they need to understand the people that are on their team.

1. **Managers need to understand that people are different.** I have heard this so many times, 'Boy if everyone on the team was like Sally, we'd be on top of everything.' Now, Sally may be great, but everyone contributes. They may contribute in different ways because everyone is different. Everyone has strengths and weaknesses. Many people have personality

traits that greatly add to their effectiveness and others have traits that hold them back a bit. People receive coaching differently, they are motivated in different ways, they learn in different ways, they have different energy levels and peak performance times. (For fun, schedule a dyed-in-the-wool morning person for the early shift with an afternoon *don't talk to me till I've had my coffee* person. Let the fun begin). That means that managers really need to get to know their people. 'I don't need to get to know my people. I have a job to do and that is to get them to do their job.' Thank you, Mr. Dictator. I am sure you will be up for manager of the year soon. I told you about the first dialysis clinic I ever ran. It was amazing how different everyone was but how they all worked together as a team. Some were just Type A, get it done people and others a bit more deliberate. Some enjoyed a lot of patient interactions, some liked doing the administrative stuff and a couple enjoyed teaching and mentoring others. A couple seemed to be looked up as the leaders and the others were quite happy just being a part of the team. The point is, they were all different and to effectively manage that group, the manager had to understand that. Many times, when I would hear about managers hiring for a position, they would say that they were looking for a, 'good fit' for that team. Does that mean someone exactly like everyone on the team? Have you ever put a puzzle together? The pieces fit perfectly together to create a great picture, but they are not all the same. Each one has a particular shape specially made to fit the pieces around it.

2. **Managers need to understand that their people are…people.** Those people on your team have families and a life outside of work. They experience problems as all of us human beings do. They face health issues, financial issues, family problems and everything else found on the great road called 'life'. They are also composed of emotions and feelings. They have good days and not so good days. Sometimes, they are up all night with a sick child or a dying relative. Managers need to remember that these people are not machines that you turn on in the morning and turn off at night. They are living, breathing, feeling, people.

The following is pretty close to an actual conversation that I was made privy to as an employee was calling in for a sick day. (It's 4:00 AM)

"Hello."

"Martha, its Jane. I am so sorry to call you, but our family has been hit with some kind of bug. I feel terrible and can't hold anything down and we had little Joey in the Emergency Room all night and just got home. There is no way I can work today. I am so sorry."

"Oh my God. Today of all days. Bill is out with his knee and Beth has to leave at noon for a funeral. I have three reports I just have to get in today not to mention a two-hour training session. I just don't know what I am going to do."

Poor Jane. She sure didn't need all of that venting. Did it automatically make Jane feel better? No. Did it help anything at all? No. Did it change the situation in anyway? No. What an insensitive, non-caring, selfish manager. I bet you a free book (well how about ½ off) that she has a problem keeping good staff members. Now, watch!

"Oh, Jane. Wow, what a rough night you had. I certainly hope you all get feeling better. Please keep me posted and let me know if we can do anything for you. Is little Joey all right?" BINGO! That manager understands that their employees are people and they have needs and do GET SICK! (I better move on. I am getting mad at the first Martha.)

Just another word here. Sometimes, employees are not as happy or energetic as they usually are. There may be something terribly wrong or they may just be having a bad day. Be understanding, but do not pry.

Wrong Way

"Jill, you seem extra quite today. Is everything OK?"

"Ya, I am good."

"I seldom see you like this, there must be something wrong."

"No, really, I am ok."

"You know, when there is a problem, it is always better to talk to someone."

"Ya, I know, I am good, really."

"People hold things in and…OK, OK! She is good. Man, I thought he would never stop.

Right way

"Jill, you seem extra quite today. Is everything OK?"

"Ya, I am good."

"Great, I am here for you and if you need anything just let me know."

"OK, thanks so much!"

Jill knows you care, and you are a good support for her if and when she needs you.

3. **Managers need to understand that people often have a hard time accepting change.** This is very important to remember because in this ever-evolving world that we live in, change is inevitable, but it is not always easy. We would do well to keep in mind the struggles we encountered stepping into a new role or being promoted to more responsibility. It wasn't easy going through that change and it is seldom easy for anyone. When I was in high school, I was not the neatest kid in the world. My room usually looked like FBI had just been there searching for clues. (If you are a guy, I bet yours wasn't much better). At seventeen and a half years old, I went to basic training and let's just say, I encountered a 'few' changes. My underclothes had to be folded in six-inch squares and neatly placed in the drawer. Uniforms had to be hung with the hangers the exact same distance apart and could not touch the sides of the closet. Boots had to be spotlessly shined. I could go on and on, but I think you get the picture. The military couldn't afford to be as supportive and gradual with change as we can be. Many recruits drop out of Basic Training because they just can't handle the change. You will lose people as well if you don't support them through the changes.

People go through several stages when learning a role. First, they are unfamiliar with any of it. Then, they start to understand the basics. This is followed by very conscious and deliberate performance. Soon, a routine is established, and confidence develops, and they eventually arrive at mastery. Guess what happens when change comes with new directions. You got it; back to square one. I hired a nurse once that had no experience in Dialysis. Dialysis was a drastic change for her from what she had been doing. She was a good nurse, so we were all very patient with her even though it took her a little longer than most to catch on. She finally got there. It wasn't long before my boss came in and announced that we were getting brand new machines. We were all so excited until we found out that it was a different type of machine. That meant learning a whole new machine. Most of them picked it up pretty quickly as we slowly integrated them onto the floor. The nurse was a bit slower and really had a hard time. Seems unfair doesn't it, all that time and effort to develop confidence working with a machine only to have it changed. She eventually got it though and was happy again.

Then a little while later, my boss came in and told us (we all hated seeing her coming) that we were going to get computers between the dialysis machines, and we were all going to learn to chart on the computers instead of paper. Oh, the groans that accompanied that announcement. But, they all (including the nurse) eventually mastered the new process and actually found it to be quite an improvement.

That was it. We never had any more changes. I see the doubt in your eyes. Yes, there were more and always will be more changes. The more you support your team through changes, the better things will be.

Patient

As someone prayed, "Lord, I need patience and I need it NOW!" We talked briefly about patience earlier but let's dig a little deeper. I think most of us have to admit that at best, we are patient some of the time. Most of the time, not so much. There are people that can be very patient but most of us are probably a little below average. I consider myself to have gotten more and more patient with age. Makes sense, I am slowing down.

I used to always seem to be in a hurry going places and inevitably would get behind a car going 45mph in a 55mph zone. As I got the chance to pass, I would look over and there he was, 100 years old, face 6 inches from the windshield, both hands had a death grip on the steering wheel. And I would think, 'Ah, what a sweet old guy. Why isn't he sitting on a porch swing drinking tea, INSTEAD OF IN FRONT OF ME?' Now (not quite 100), as I get passed and looked at, I wonder what they are saying.

We are going to look briefly at three areas where managers need to be patient. I am sure you can think of more, but I think these three are particularly vital for managers.

1. **Managers need to be patient with themselves.** We all know that there are a lot more variables in dealing with people than other things that we manage. The human element can produce tremendous results,

but there are times that it also requires patience in waiting for the results to develop. The first person that a manager has to be patient with is themselves. As a manager, you have to give yourself time to accomplish your goals. Rome wasn't built is a day and you won't reach all your goals in a day either. When you get impatient with yourself, bad things start to happen. When you are not patient with yourself, it often converts to impatience with your team. We will discuss that a little more later. Secondly, doubts start to roll in. 'Can I really do this? Am I really the right person for this job? I wonder what my manager is thinking about me?' On that last question, I have found that conscientious people are much harder and more demanding on themselves than their supervisors. Give yourself time. Remember that person that wanted that job so badly and was going to really make a difference; you are still there. Here is a truth that I think will help. Please remember to do this and it will help you be more patient with yourself.

2. **Make sure you always differentiate between long- and short-term goals.** Frustration comes when you give yourself short term expectation for long term goals. Let me illustrate. You are now a sales manager in a big company with a team of seven salespeople. Your goal is for your team to climb to number ONE in the company and that is a tremendous goal indeed. You are currently forth

out of 10 teams. The following month, you are still forth. The next month, you moved up to third. 'This is taking too long. We should be doing better than this. Bill, your numbers are down; is there a problem. Sally, are you seriously taking a week off in the middle of this big campaign? Harry, do you really need surgery on that wrist?' So, you can see, your personal impatience has now produced impatience in your team, and you are doing and saying things that could really be devastating to the relationships that you have worked so long to build. Set short term, attainable goals that you can celebrate with your team when reached, while continuing the vision or the long term stretch goal. Be patient with yourself and it will help you systematically reach your goals.

I started a notebook when I first started managing a Medical Aid Station in England. One of the sections I entitled, 'Management Mistakes'. Needless to say, I could write another book just from that section of the notebook (Just a short book; a short story; an article; oh okay, a NOVEL). I was so glad I did as I have used it to fashion and improve my leadership and also to help others learn the ropes. Had I not been patient with myself, many of those mistakes could have made me want to quit managing. Let me throw this in for you baseball fans. A .333 Batting Average is actually pretty good. The majority of major league players don't hit at that level. Do you know what that average represents? The player gets a hit one out of three at bats. If he gets one hit every three times up, he will have that GOOD average. That means he is getting <u>out</u> two out of three times. Baseball is a bit different. I hope you get more than one out of three things right. But, the point is the same. You have to be patient.

3. **Thirdly, you have to be patient with those on your team**. Sally is going to be refreshed and ready to hit it hard when she gets back from vacation. Everyone needs a break (especially managers by the way). Harry's been in pain so long with that wrist that getting it fixed will help him to get back to top form again. People work at different levels, they learn at different paces, and it takes time to develop the people you have into being what you want them to be. The first few smashes of a sculptor's hammer don't produce much. The first few strokes of a painter's brush don't look that great; but when they are finished, a masterpiece will appear. **It takes time.** I saw this so many times and you probably have too, and it so illustrates what I am trying to say. Karen and Terri have been technicians for over fifteen years now. Their friend Janice had also been there a while and recently retired. The manager hired a new girl, Glenda. Glenda was a hard worker and very willing to learn the new job at which she had no experience. The first few weeks went by and Glenda was learning pretty quickly. In just a few more weeks, she was able to perform much of her role on her own, with

minimal supervision. Glenda was a very thorough and conscientious person and was a bit slower than the others as she wanted to make sure she wasn't missing anything. Then, it started.

"I just don't know if she is going to make it. She is slow as molasses. Some people just can't keep up with the fast pace that we have to work here."

"Ya, the boss might have to start looking for someone else." Are you laughing yet? Do I have some Karens and Terrys reading this? Gotcha! They have been doing their job for over ten years and expect Glenda to be at that pace in six weeks. I am sure the others took longer than six weeks to get to the efficiency that they had developed. I am hoping as a manager you realize this vital point, but be patient with those that are on your team. Years and years of pressurizing coal (carbon) will produce beautiful diamonds. You may have some diamonds there, be patient.

Temperate (Self Control)

It is very important for a manager to always remain in control of themselves in order to control what is going on. Losing self-control often times will disenable you from using the tools that are at your disposal, like critical thinking and making sound judgements. Let me make a few statements that I hope you will ponder on for a bit. No one can make you angry. People can do things that would warrant anger, but you are the one that chooses whether or not to get angry. No one can discourage you. They can do discouraging things and produce discouraging situations but again, the choice is yours. That is what self-control is all about.

A leader with self-control has a solid decision-making process. (More detail on that in my book, 'Reincarnate Now'). That decision-making process allows them to take clear, rational ACTIONS. When you lose self-control, you go from taking appropriate ACTIONS to making REACTIONS, often without thinking them through.

You all know how verbal skirmishes take place. They are mad and say something and so you get mad and say something back and on it goes. As a manager, you do not have the luxury to participate in that. In these situations, you need to, like some say, 'Hit the PAUSE button,' or 'Take a Timeout.' Slow things way down and deescalate to the point that you will not permit yourself to get angry. Then, think each action and statement out clearly after sufficient consideration.

I do not know how many meetings I have stopped abruptly because emotions and tempers erupted, and everyone was losing self-control. I basically said that we would not be able to accomplish anything constructively as long as we were not able to think clearly and make good decisions. We rescheduled the meeting and I worked with the teammates individually to ensure the next meeting would not be a repeat.

The key is this; as a leader you have many great qualities that are a part of your internal makeup. When you are able to interpret events properly, those internal drivers will help you act and speak appropriately. When you choose to react, you no longer have those drivers available to you and your actions are really just reactions to the events.

Self-Control is also very important in day-to-day operations when the manager is going through personal issues. It is easy to say that we need to leave home at home when we get to work, but it is a lot more difficult to function at top level while being weighed down by personal issues. As we discussed earlier, managers are people and life happens to us all. Remember this, **transparency—minus in-depth detail—with the team is crucial during these times**. That will help eliminate any incorrect perceptions.

Mark, the manager comes to work and seems very quiet and a bit distracted. Cathy approached him about needing to take a day off to take her daughter to a specialist for her ears. Mark didn't mind a bit, but his demeanor made Cathy feel that he was unhappy over the request.

Mark added to his approval of the day off, "Hey, don't mind me. I am a bit off my A game today. I have some things going on and I am a bit distracted. But, it's all good. Thanks for understanding."

Cathy is not only relieved that he was not upset but will now also be a little extra supportive of her boss. She, like everyone, knows life happens to us all. Notice Mark didn't go into detail. Human nature wants us to divulge the details to get some sympathy. If you don't believe me, spend a little time in the doctor's office waiting room.

"... then I had to have my gallbladder taken out, boy was I sick with that. And my rheumatism was acting up. I could hardly change my oxygen tank out. I have to be on that for my breathing and... ... ..." I think you get the idea. (If anyone is ever doing that with you, just say 'oh my!' after each thing. That will keep the conversation going.)

As managers, you cannot go into detail. Just let them know you are alright but are dealing with some personal things. They will understand.

A Communicator

Relationships are vital to the manager and the key to developing good relationships is communication. A lot of times when we talk about someone being a good communicator, we think about their ability to speak to individuals or to large audiences. Communication is a two-way process and, in my opinion, the more difficult and more important of the two is **listening and hearing**. These two terms sound alike but are quite different.

When people talk to us, they are trying to convey a message. Listening simply means that we are listening to what they are saying. Hearing means, and we often say, 'Ya, I hear you there,' that not only are we listening to the words, but we are hearing the message. Here is just a little example.

"Hey Boss, you got a minute?"

"No, I am the manager and a very busy person. I will try and squeeze you in sometime next week when..." (Ha, just trying to see if you were really listening.)

"Hey Boss, you got a minute?"

"I always have time for you, Chuck. What's up?"

"It is really getting crazy out there. I mean we are constantly going full blast, and some are skipping breaks and shortening their lunch time just to keep up. I know we are shorthanded but it's starting to take its toll on all of us. No one wants to complain but I thought I should let you know how we feel."

Now, the manager listened intently to every word. He **listened to the facts**. But, he also **heard the message** that something needed to be done to support the team. Don't just listen to what they are saying, make sure you identify the message.

Let's go a step further. As we mentioned, it is vitally important that you identify the message but just as important to ensure that they know that you got the message. I have talked to a few of my managers and when I was finished, I know they listened but didn't hear me. 'Went in one ear and out the other.' To make sure the other party knows you got the message, it is good to identify and reflect back to them what you heard.

"I am hearing you say that we really need more hands-on deck out there to keep everyone from burning out. I just wanted to make sure I we were on the same page." That little statement right there will do more to build the confidence they have in you as a leader than you can imagine. You listened and you heard them. Just a few more comments on communicating.

1. Check on the privacy of the conversation before beginning. A simple, "Do you want to talk here or go somewhere private?" gives them the choice and also makes them feel that you really are going to

be present in the conversation. Not just a, "Ya sure, what do you need? I am on my way to the front." That may make them wonder just how in tune to the conversation you will be.

2. If you feel it is an important issue or a very detailed one, ask permission to take a few private notes so that you can recap at the end. This is another way to show them that you are intent on addressing any issues presented.

3. Give them your undivided attention. Turn the computer monitor off so that you are not tempted to see the last e-mail that came in. Turn your cell phone off and ask the secretary to hold your calls. Once all this is done, they are certain you are going to take this conversation very seriously. I had a one-on-one meeting scheduled with my upline manager once. I had an agenda of the things I needed to discuss with her prepared. I arrived early and patiently waited 20 minutes past our scheduled start time. I only had forty minutes left when I finally got in to see her and still had an hour's worth of things to cover. During that meeting, she constantly watched her computer, answered two calls, and stopped the meeting so she could go out in the lobby to talk to someone she deemed as very important. Finally, I got up and told her I would rebook the appointment during a time she could listen. I left that office feeling like the most insignificant person on earth. Please, don't make that mistake. Give everyone your full attention.

4. At the end, review the conversation with them to make sure you got all the high points. Don't be afraid to refer to your notes. As they leave, they should be saying to themselves, 'I believe he got it'.

5. We are all guilty of this next one and I assure you, it can really muddle up the message. Don't start formulating replies in your head until you have fully heard them out. I am HORRIBLE at that. As soon as I start to hear the issues, answers start popping up in my mind. It really takes training to be an effective, FOCUSED listener. As you start formulating your, 'save the day', master plan in your mind, they are saying other things that you are missing. Here is a good illustration. You may not think it is a good one, but I do, and I am writing the book, so I win. 'Yes, but I bought this book, so I should have a say.' If you would quit arguing with me, we could get back to where we were. So…now I forgot where we were… oh, *ya*. Here is a good illustration of what I am trying to say. Rick comes in to see the boss at a car wash station.

    "Boss, you have to do something about Carl. He is so slow. I have done six cars today and he has done four. We both get paid the same, so I don't think that is fair." At this point, your mind goes BING. 'How can I get a fire under Carl? Does he need more training? Is he just loafing a bit? I guess I could have the floor supervisor watch him for…' See, you are already formulating a plan. What you didn't hear Rick say was, '...and it's because he does all that extra stuff. He goes around the car with a rag and makes sure all the extra wax is wiped off and he buffs up the headlights a bit and checks the windshield wipers and...' Now, you missed all that while you are thinking of a reply. Carl isn't slow, he is very conscientious and doing above what is expected. That would make the customers very happy. Listen and HEAR the entire message before you start thinking about a resolution.

6. Lastly, watch your non-verbal communications. Your body language can say a lot and either help or hinder your communications. Good, direct eye contact and an occasional nod means you are listening and very engaged. Lack of eye contact, crossing your arms, and taking frequent deep sighs say just the opposite. Also, watch the eye rolling. It is not as easy as you think, especially if you really disagree with something. Just remember; they hear you, but they also see you.

I am sure you can think of many more desirable qualities for managers to possess. I just wanted to review the ones that I think are vital to a manger's success. Again, you can't learn these traits, but you can develop them. It's like the time I read a book on speed reading. It took me forever to get through that book.

CHAPTER 4

HIRING GOOD PEOPLE

This chapter is dealing with the one thing you really have to do in order to build a good team. The key is to **hire right, train well, and keep the good ones.** Simple right? Well, not really. I told you about some of the struggles I had managing my first dialysis clinic. After a few months, the only one from the original team left was my secretary. Most of the original people there were the 'Wrong Stuff'. Over the next two years, I hired some good quality people, trained them properly, and they stayed for years. I believe that was really the turning point for that clinic.

Hiring has become a very difficult process. It seems like the more advanced we get with our interviewing process; the more skillful people have become in being interviewed. I mean, I think there are some professional interviewees out there. They know all the right answers to the questions.

Every manager has their own interviewing style. I just want to share a few things about how I run my interviews. I divide my interviews up into four segments. The Initial interview that I do alone, the Subsequent interview with some of the team, the shadowing period, and the Final interview. I also divide up the initial interview up into two stages; 'Are you right for the team?' and 'Is the job and team right for you?'

I have been invited to sit in on many interviews where it was always hard for me to keep quiet. I was often amazed how most of them started out. "Well, we start at 6:00 AM and work ten-hour shifts. Are you Ok with that? Sometimes, we have to work a little later but not too often. You will be training here for about a week here and then you have to go to Richmond for a week of training. Is that OK with you? Once you are fully trained, you will be on call for one evening a week and one weekend a month. Sometimes, it is kind of fast paced, are you OK with that?

Why don't they just ask them the two main questions, 'When can you start?' and 'Can you pass a drug test?'

In the first segment of my interview process, I am trying to decide if this candidate would be a good fit for the position. I do not go over much about the position but rather dig into who they are as a person. I have already reviewed their resume and checked their references to even get to this point.

All the questions I ask are open ended questions that cannot be answered in one or two words.

'Have you ever gone above and beyond to help a patient with a need?' This is a closed ended question that they can answer with one word and of course it would be, YES!

'Tell me about a time that you went above and beyond to help a patient with a need.' This is an open-ended question that requires relaying a past experience. When asking an open-ended question.

1. Don't penalize them for a pause. They will want to think of the best example. Sometimes, it takes a minute or two to decide.

2. Don't interrupt the silence. This happens all the time. Interviewers add additional information, explain the question in more detail, and prod them along. If they need more information about the question, they will ask. Let silence work. *'Tell me about a time that you went above and beyond to help a patient with a need.'* (PAUSE) *'Just some time that you really did more than required to help a patient.'* (PAUSE) *'It can be anytime in your nursing career.'* (DON'T PROD)

3. You can if you want to, but I avoid some of the standard questions that everyone has a textbook answer for. 'What do you feel are your greatest strengths?' Ask on your next interview and see if you don't get something like this. 'I am a real people person and a team player. I have a strong work ethic and learn new things quickly.' (If I only had a nickel for every time I heard that answer). And almost always the, 'What would you consider your area of greatest improvement opportunity', question is answered, 'I need to brush up a bit on my computer skills with all the new things out and I have trouble delegating sometimes. I like to do it all myself.'

4. If you do ask those questions, follow up with examples. 'You say you are a team player. Give me an example of a time that you worked together with others as a team to accomplish a task'. 'Give me an example of something different to you that you had to learn and describe your process for learning it'. You want to get inside these people and see what they really are and not just what they say they are.

Allen M. Daugherty

There are other things to keep in mind while you are interviewing. People that have been in their positions for years may not present as polished interviewers and their resumes may not be literary works of art, but they may be great for the job. Once, I interviewed a nurse that had worked in a hospital for sixteen years. Her mother had been on dialysis and she was intrigued, so she applied for the job. Her resume was acceptable but very old fashioned and the interview was a bit awkward, but I hired her, and she became a great dialysis nurse. I kept in mind that she had not interviewed for a position for over sixteen years.

Others come in with quite a bit of experience…in interviewing. They are really good at it because they have done it so often. They have had several recent jobs and would probably start applying for other positions as soon as you hire them. I call that a RED FLAG.

Back to the process. After the first stage of the interview, I make a decision. I have three options.

1. **I like what I have seen so far, so I will continue with the second stage.** I transition like this, 'Marsha, I like what I have seen so far and would like to continue on with the second part of the interview where I give you some details about the position. You can tell me what you think, and I will answer any questions that you may have. Are you okay with continuing?

2. **I have some reservations but have not totally ruled this candidate out.** In this case, I simply thank for

their time, and tell them that I may be calling them back for the second part of the interview. These are people that I probably won't hire but may give them a second chance after interviewing others.

3. **This is not the candidate I want.** Here, I simply tell them that I appreciate them applying and taking the time to come in, but I don't feel that they would be a good fit for the position. Many managers give the standard, 'I call and let you know when I have made my decision.' That is usually because they want to avoid face to face confrontation. Think about it, why waste the time they have to seek another position, waiting for your call. Close the book.

I then have the candidates that made it through both stages of the first interview come in for the second interview with some of the team members. This gives them a chance to meet some of the people that they might be working with and gives the team a chance to meet the candidate. I spend some time with the teammates that will be doing the interview to go over some ground rules and make suggestions on the interview process itself. Although I am directing this interview, I do not participate much. I let the team do the interviewing.

I do, however, ask them to limit themselves to a set number of questions a piece and I ask them to submit their questions to me in advance so I can review them for legal purposes. I have gotten many chuckles over some of the questions the team has come up with. I make some opening remarks and let the interview roll.

The next day, we meet to discuss the interview. I ask each one for positive notes they made about the candidate and any negative ones that they make have. I NEVER ask them for a yes or no on the candidate. I value their feedback but ultimately, I have to make the decision, plus I do not want them getting into a debate and affect the cohesion that they have amongst themselves.

If I decide to go to the next step, I ask the candidate to come in and shadow others that are in the role that she is applying for. It is usually about four hours, centered around lunch and the busiest time of the day. I want them to see the role at its busiest, so they know what to expect.

I have to tell you this story of when I interviewed for my first dialysis job. I was working EMS on the ambulance, lifted a very heavy patient and got a hernia. I had it repaired and went home the same day. The dialysis techs were always telling me to apply for a position that had opened and work with them. I had applied and got called for an interview the day after my surgery.

I arrived at the center, walking slowly and a bit stooped over (and on Percocet). I explained what had happened and the interview went very well. The manager walked me around and showed me the floor. The nurses were sitting at the desk, the techs were just walking around checking on things, most of the patients were asleep in their chairs. Wow, what a piece of cake job. I got hired and arrived a few weeks later for my first day. I got there at 8:00AM and all was nice and quiet as when I had interviewed.

But when 9:30AM hit, it turned into pandemonium. It was about an hour and a half hour stretch when they took all the patients off and the next shift on the machines. I watched in awe wondering if I could ever do that. When you have someone come into shadow, let them experience the busiest time. It's only fair to them.

I recommend buying lunch for everyone to give the candidate a chance to eat lunch with some of the team. This gives everyone a chance to get to know them a bit and the candidate, a chance to ask any questions that they may have. Once again, I talk to the team after the candidate leaves for comments. I do not ask for recommendations, just comments or concerns (Although you always have a few that will give you a thumbs up if they like the candidate).

I had a young lady come in for a dialysis technician interview once and she was really chomping at the bits to get the job. She asked if she could just look around to see exactly what we did. I started walking her through the clinic past several patients that were dialyzing. I was telling her a little bit about how the machines work when I heard a bit of a groan. I turned to find her on the floor. She has passed out when she saw all the blood circulating through the blood lines.

I picked her up and carried her to a reclinable chair in a separate room and she recovered pretty quickly. I had to laugh as she looked at me and asked, "So, I guess I will not be getting this job?" It is always good to allow the candidate to see exactly what they will be doing.

The final interview starts off with a general conversation, answering any questions that may arise. Then, I go over the hiring and training process and basic expectations. I present them with the offer, show them the benefits package, and ask if they have any further questions. I tell the candidate they can accept on the spot or they have up to 2 business days to let me know if they want to think it over. If they accept on the spot, we agree on a start date and get things rolling.

CHAPTER 5

KEEPING GOOD PEOPLE

Retaining good employees is not always easy, but it is very crucial in developing any successes you may have as a manager. Managers are very busy people, and I cannot stress enough how important it is to spend time 'working' on retention. I bet you don't see that penciled in many calendars. I know, you are saying, 'Well, I am doing that all the time.' It will benefit you tremendously if you spend some time periodically thinking of ways to keep your good people. Just a few general comments to get started.

1. Performance in the workplace is always better with tenured staff. If your workplace is like a revolving door for employees, you do not have time to develop them into the A Team you need to reach your goals. A good manager studies their people and works to capitalize and develop their strengths and to improve any weakness. This takes time and you will not be very successful if they are only with you for a year.

2. Taking the time and energy to retain good staff is time well spent as opposed to all the time you'll have to spend resourcing, advertising, interviewing, hiring, and training new people. Things have been tense at work with one employee out sick. Everyone, including you, has been working very hard. Here is

a good place to stop and think, what can I do for the team to show them how much I appreciate them. It's not that most managers don't appreciate their teams, it is that they just don't think about showing it.

3. Even if there are some financial considerations involved, it will be well worth it in the long run. Many managers are not able to initiate things like raises and bonuses as they are handled further upline. You can certainly do a lot of lobbying for them though. I always added some numbers to my lobbying efforts. For example, an underpaid dialysis nurse tells you they are looking at another position because they will get $1.50 more an hour. The math is like this. $1.50 an hour is about $3,000 a year. It cost over $30,000 to hire and train a new nurse. You can't do it all the time to everyone but if you really want it, show them some compelling reasons with financial backing. Some things you can do that may seem little but go a long way in building a solid relationship with your team include buying lunches occasionally and presenting some awards. Doughnuts, (They are not just for the police), snacks, and other things along this line really do show you care.

Many people think that most employees leave a position to get more money or better benefits with another job. The truth is that the number one reason people leave their jobs is the relationship (or lack of) they have with their managers. Think about the great leaders of our time and how those under them followed them into adversity, battle and sometimes even seemingly hopeless situations. All because they were loyal to a leader that was worthy to be followed.

On a more practical level, there are many employees that are offered better positions with better incentives for more money and would not even consider it; because of the allegiance they have formed with their leader. On the other hand, there are employees who apply for any opportunities that arise, sometimes even taking a cut in pay to get out of their current workplace' mostly because of the dissatisfaction they have with their manager.

As I said earlier, there are scores of great books out there on leadership that dive pretty deep into this one subject and I would recommend reading them. I just want to share a few points on this topic from my perspective and experience. No big revelations here, but I think you will agree they are essential.

1. Work hard to develop the leadership qualities that we mentioned earlier (Copy from the Table of Contents). I have that list of qualities and a few more written in a notebook and when I was a manager, I reviewed them constantly. Just reading them repeatedly and assessing your success in those areas can help you improve all through your leadership career. I remember thinking about dependability once and it was during a time when we were so busy. I had put some things the team had asked about on the 'back burner'. I realized that I needed to really

focus on those things in order to be truly dependable. Reviewing the list helps. Just a note on the 'back burner'. Things on the back burner can burn or boil over just as easily as things on the front burner *if they are not attended to*. (To be sure, I tried it at home and wow, what a mess. I am still in the doghouse. The things writers do to make sure we are accurate).

2. Your mission and your values should not just be things that you implore others to do. You have to live them for order for them to have any power. You can talk a good talk, but if it is not backed up by actions, it's like a tire without air, it won't get you very far. I am speaking personally now, I can tolerate mistakes, judgment errors and many other things but I have a real issue with people who say one thing and do another; people who talk the talk but don't walk the talk.

"They say that the employees are their top priority, but the manager sure doesn't act that way."

"They tell us they value our ideas. I have given the manager several ideas and I have never heard anything back."

"All this talk about teamwork but the manager is never out here when we need him."

I think you get the idea. If it is your credo or the company's mission. Put it to practice and just not talk about it.

3. Here is a really valuable yet simple piece of advice on the matter of retention that you can get. Look back at your past managers. Jot down all the things that they did that made you feel really special. The things that they did that made you glad that they were your manager. Think hard and try not to miss even the little things. Those are the same things that you can do to help your team feel the same way. On the other hand, do the same thing with things that upset you or that you were very unhappy with. Some things could be from the same manager but not usually. Again, capture even the little things. You will see just how important they were in the way that they made you feel.

On December 24th, 1999, I was working on a patient when my supervisor, Lenise Sypult, came and told me that she would take over for me. She said my wife had called, very upset and that I needed to go home. My twenty-one-year-old son had unexpectedly died in the night for no apparent cause. When we got to the hospital, the doctor told us that there was nothing they could do and that he indeed, was gone. I don't need to tell you what a heartbreak that was. I looked through the window from the counselling room and saw Lenise outside. She stayed with me until I left to go home. She was so supportive the entire time, came to the funeral, and was especially helpful when I returned to work. She cared, and that stuck with me more than anything else any other manager had ever done.

After completing both lists, the next step is obvious; incorporate the positive things into your leadership while avoiding the negatives like a plague. You will be amazed at how much this exercise and some self-reflection will improve how your employees will feel about you.

I want you to do something else as well. I did this with several of my managers once, in an effort to improve retention. Buy a small plant and put it in your office or somewhere at the workplace. You need to water it and perhaps give it some plant food occasionally. You need to place it where it gets some sunlight. In short, you need to pay attention to this plant if it is going to thrive. The same goes with retention. If you don't think about it and you don't do anything for it, you can expect to lose some employees.

I guarantee that the time and effort you put into retention will be paid back to you many times over. It is time and energy well spent. Was my manager busy on that day my son died? Yep. Did she have other things that she needed to do? Certainly, but she took the time to care and that goes a long way. When I think back to all the managers I have ever had, she will always be the best! Want a great rule to live by? **Become the type of leader that you would love working for.**

CHAPTER 6

DEALING WITH PROBLEMS

Wouldn't it be nice if we could manage a team and never have any problems? It would, but there is no Wizard behind the curtain (If you are young, ask someone older what that means). Problems will arise and that is when your true leadership capabilities are tested and hopefully proven. It is the rough sea that tests the sailor, the fiercest battles test the soldiers, and problems that come up will test you.

Problems are so common that we actually start looking for them. Some of you have probably done this a time or two. I can remember sitting in my office one day after about a month of one thing after another crisis came along. All was calm and everything was running smoothly. I said to myself, "Okay, what is coming next and when?" Then, I laughed. Enjoy the good times while you can and recharge your batteries.

Notice the title of the chapter starts with 'Dealing with'. Not putting problems off or ignoring problems, but dealing with them. I cannot stress this enough. It is ALWAYS better to deal with problems early than to wait until they become bigger and harder to manage.

I got a fishing hook stuck deep into my thumb once. I took it out, cleaned it up and carried on. The next day it was a bit red, so I put some ointment on it and carried on. The next day it was red, hot and swollen, so I soaked it in some stuff

I had bought and carried on. The next day there was a red streak along the underside of my arm, and I didn't carry on. Two days later and massive IV antibiotic therapy, I got out of the hospital. The moral of the story is, fishing is dangerous. No, it is the fact that if things are handled PROPERLY, early, they won't cause you more trouble down the road.

I heard a manager say once that he let most issues go for a while to see if they would resolve themselves without his intervention. There may be a few instances when some problems will resolve themselves but not many and you better keep a close eye on them. I had a couple of employees get into a little spat. They separately came into my office and vented. My first advice was for them to try and talk their differences out. The next day, I went out to see how things were going and they were in the break room cutting up and having a good time together.

I have had the same thing happen with other employees where I could see that they were not making any progress, so I did intervene. Here is a great question for you. *Does a roof only leak when it is raining?* Well, truthfully, the answer is yes. Follow up question; Does that mean that there is only a hole in the roof when it is raining? The answer is, of course, no. And I know from experience that it is a lot better to fix a hole in a roof when it is not raining. Tremendous lesson here; take care of the problems even if for the minute they aren't actively causing issues.

I had notified one of our technical people about an issue we were having in our water room. It was a small leak around a valve. He came in to look at it and said he had to order a part and would replace it as soon as it got in. I called to double check on a Friday and the part had gotten in, but he was 'tied up' and could not get to us until Monday.

I usually went to the office for a bit on Sunday evenings just to make sure everything was good to go for Monday morning. When I got to the center, I noticed that the light blue carpet in the lobby was now dark blue. Well, it wasn't dark blue, it was under a couple inches of water. You got it, the valve broke and flooded the entire building. What a mess. I had to call everyone in to get the water out, he had to come in to replace the valve, we had to get a company in to help fry the building out. To make a long story short, we worked all night to get the clinic ready for patients in the morning and then we all worked that day. If he had only…Get the picture?

Personnel problems always seem to be the hardest to deal with. I want to make this very clear; if you have problems with confrontation, you have got to do whatever it takes to get over it. Confrontation is not in many of our comfort zones but is usually necessary when dealing with people. Managers fall into many poor leadership practices trying to avoid confrontation. A very common one goes something like this. I had a manager working for me that hated confronting her employees when an issue arose. Instead of addressing the issue directly with them, she would post a notice on the Communication Board addressing the issue (not the person involved) and made EVERYONE sign it.

For example, Katie has been failing to stock her section before going home in the evening. That made it much harder for those starting the next morning to get going. It was brought to the attention of the manager a few times and finally she posted a note on the bulletin board concerning that very subject and asked all the staff to sign it. Although Katie had to read and sign it and probably got the message, the rest of the team that did their stocking, should not have had to. It was done that way, yep, you got it, to avoid confrontation.

After this happens a few times, the manager will be branded as someone that is afraid to confront people with issues and that is a very undesirable characteristic to have as a manager.

Another way confrontation is avoided is by just letting issues go in hopes that they will correct themselves. When the manager was first informed of this situation, she asked the others if they had mentioned it to her as she perhaps just forgets. They had reminded her several times, but it continued to happen. Once this goes on for a while with no managerial intervention, the manager will be branded as someone that, 'just lets problems go', Soon, the theme will be, 'There is no use telling the manager, she won't do anything about it anyhow.' This is not the kind of leader that will earn confidence and respect from the team.

There are so many great leadership books out there that give great insight into dealing with employee issues and I recommend that you read as many of them as you can.

NOTE: I cannot stress enough how important it is for leaders to read and learn every day to enhance their leadership skills. When you don't, you just have what you currently know to operate on. When you read and research, you will have so much more available to you.

When I deal with someone, I use a mental template that I have compiled from several experts on the subject. In a simple format, it goes like this:

1. Set the atmosphere. (Phone and computer off, private place, no interruptions, plenty of time allotted, etc.)
2. Try to set the employee a bit at ease as a trip to the office is usually an indication that it's time to raise the defense shields
3. Thoroughly discuss the issue with the employee
4. Ask the employee if they understand what has been explained
5. Ask the employee for their input into the situation
6. Describe, in detail, the expectations and offer solutions if possible.
7. Agree on a plan to correct the issue
8. Schedule a follow up meeting to review progress.

Let's watch this approach to the previous issue.

"Hey, Katie, can I talk to you in my office for a minute?"

"Sure, be right in."

"Please forgive the office if it is a bit cluttered. I am working on something and I like to spread things out all over so that I can see it all. Do you do that?"

"Ha, ha, no I just have the clutter without the reason."

"Ya, right. I bet your house is immaculate."

"Actually, my husband is pretty neat, but I have a time trying to keep up with the three little ones."

"I bet. Are there two in school now?

"Yes, the third one starts next year."

"Wow, they sure grow up fast."

"Yes, they do."

"Katie, I just wanted to explain something to you and see if you understand the importance of it. One of the duties of the technicians, is to stock their section before they leave. Have you been doing this in your section?"

"Oh, the others must have said something. I just told myself today that I have to really doublecheck things before I go home. I admit I have been forgetting. My bad and I will apologize to the others."

"So, I am hearing you say that you are just having some trouble remembering to check things at the end of the day, right?"

"Yes, I always keep some things stocked up but forget some other things."

"I am so glad we are on the same page. The reason we made that as a required duty as there are so many things that can happen first thing in the morning and having to run to the back for supplies makes it worse. I think you agree."

"Yes, I certainly do, and it won't happen again."

"I trust that you got this but just as a small suggestion, perhaps put a note on your locker, maybe even a comic one like 'GOT STOCKED' like the Got Milk commercials."

"Ha, ha, that is good. Yes, I will think of something. That really is a good idea."

"Wonderful and thanks for talking this out with me. Let's check in next week to make sure we got this covered, OK?"

"Sure, sorry again."

"No problem, I have to be reminded to do things also. See ya."

Obviously, everything went very well here, and it doesn't always happen that way. The key is having a pretty simple agenda to make sure you cover all the key points. Preparation for important things in life trumps 'winging it', every time.

She is not very happy and has been looking for another job. She is a wiz with the computer and is very tech savvy. She can make a spreadsheet up for anything. Bill on the other hand, is what you would call a well caffeinated employee. It is hard to get him to stay still for anything. He does report out on several items with rather basic (being very kind here) charts and graphs. Yes, you hit it. With just a little rearranging of some of the tasks, the manager has improved his section and the individual members of the team.

This is again a little corny but **getting to know the strengths of your people and capitalizing on them is invaluable.** In this example, we got the right people doing the right thing and they all worked it out as a team. It is hardly ever that easy, but the point is the same.

In the nursing field, I always closely observed and got to know my employees very well. Some were good at teaching. I had them doing most of the training for our new folks. Some were leaders and were placed in charge of various sections. Some were faster and thrived on staying busy, others a bit more deliberate and enjoyed spending a little extra time with patients. Whatever the case, find the qualities in your people that make them tick and use it to the fullest. It will benefit them and you.

No matter how high the octane is in a gasoline product, it won't perform well in a diesel engine. I said that to say... now, why did I say that? Oh, ya, no matter how good a person is at something, unless they are in the right role, they won't flourish. If they are operating well below what they are capable of and their expertise is not being utilized, they will stagnate, get bored and probably, eventually leave. If they are given a role above their capabilities, they will probably try their best but fail.

This is kind of funny, but it illustrates what I am getting at. I worked in a diner when I was in high school. When I first got there, there was a dishwasher working there that wanted to be a cook. He had previously been a cook, but the diner just had an opening for a dishwasher, so he took it. He complained all the time, said he could cook better than the cooks we had and one day, he just didn't show up and we never saw him again.

About a year later, we had plenty of dishwashers and by then I was washing dishes and cooking. We lost a couple of cooks in a short period of time and then 'made' one of the dishwashers a cook. He didn't know how to fry an egg. He shadowed with me for a shift and I told the manger it was a mistake to have him cook on his own for quite some time, but you know how things go. One shift, numerous complaints, mad customers (and waitresses) and he was gone. The right person in the right role is the ticket.

There are occasions when an employee isn't just working out. Some managers, especially the ones that don't like confrontation, (that's a poor choice of terms; none of us like confrontation)…especially managers that won't confront issues. That is really bad for morale and managers that do that lose the respect of their people. Sometimes, you have to pull a weed to save the garden.

I try to divide performance issues into two categories; **can't** and **won't**. The question is, can't the employee do it properly or won't they do it properly? Can't then, can be divided into two sub-categories; they can't because they need more training, or they just can't handle the expectations of the job. I have made a habit in the past of putting those in the 'can't' category with a mentor for a while to identify any areas that more training is needed. We then develop a re-training plan and evaluate progress weekly.

If there is no improvement, they most likely just can't. It is really hard to let these folks go because they try so hard to get it but are just not able. It is not fair to them to be asked to continue in a job where they are not able to perform the tasks. If there is improvement, then moderate monitoring should continue until the employee is very comfortable and competent.

The ones that won't are more of a discipline problem than a training problem. Some want to do it their way in their good time and they are there just to collect a paycheck. I have a little less trouble letting go of these folks. I spend a lot of time with them and give them several chances. There comes a time when no improvement is made, or actions are going to produce consequences that necessitate a solid judgement.

My rule has always been this; have I, the manager, done everything I can do to turn this person around? If the answer is no, then I go back to the drawing board. If I cannot, after conferring with other managers, come up with anything else that could possibly be done, I make the call. Please, make sure you only issue one, *final warning*. I have seen managers say to someone, 'This is your last chance.' but it really wasn't. Your word here is important so make sure you hold your ground.

I just want to make a few comments on handling problems in general. I must sound like a broken record, but there are tons of books available that can give you really good insight on problem solving so check them out. I want to review some very practical things here that have been a help to me.

1. Problems never come at a good time (that is because there is never a good time to have a problem). They have to be correctly prioritized with the rest of your operations. The key question then here is, 'Will this problem affect our operations and interfere with completing our mission?' If the answer is yes, it would then require top prioritization. If no, then it should be prioritized with the other things that you are doing. Here is an example that shows both sides. You have a contract with a groundskeeping service. It is fall, there are leaves everywhere, the grass has not been cut, and the shrubs need trimming. You called the groundskeeping service, but they have not responded. Time for a meeting to discuss the contract. Your calendar is booked with several pressing issues for the entire week. Is the groundskeeping an issue that affects operations? No! So that should be booked in when possible. Now, it is winter, and you just had a pretty significant storm with snow and ice. The grounds company has not come around to plow and salt the entrance and parking lot as indicated in the contract. Employees, visitors and customers could be at risk with the slippery conditions. Will this affect

operations? Yes! This now takes top priority. Just a simple illustration, but I think you get the idea.

2. Make sure you get all the details when presented with a problem. It is well worth your time to investigate and do what I call a 'deep dive' into problems. Sometimes, we treat symptoms but don't treat the illness. Many years ago, I went out to start my car one day and the battery was dead. It was old so I replaced it and it started up fine for a while. Then, it happened again. I recharged the battery, and it was fine for a while and then dead again. The next step was the alternator, then the voltage regulator. Finally, I swallowed my pride and took it to an auto-electrical place to get it checked out. He hooked a meter up and said the battery was being drained. He followed it the whole way to the light in the trunk that had a short. Replace that $.75 bulb (told you it was a few years ago) and that fixed it. Always look for the root of the problem and all the contributing factors so that you totally understand just what the problem is. A small physician office was experiencing a drop in appointments. The office manager initially shrugged it off as an up and down experience, but the number of appointments never rebounded. She wondered if perhaps the people were having an issue with the doctor, but everyone she talked to just loved him. Finally, she did some surveys of present and past patients. A root cause surfaced, 'Too long of a wait time. Physician always running late.' She talked

to the nurses who assured her that unless it was an unusual circumstance, the doctor was normally right on time or just a few minutes late. After a little more digging, the manager discovered that the secretary was asking everyone to come in 30 minutes before their appointment time in case they need to fill out paperwork. So, for a 9:30AM appointment, she told them that the appointment was for 9:00 AM. Since most people come in a bit early anyhow, some were waiting almost an hour to see the doctor. Problem identified.

3. Then, make sure you have all the options for resolving the problem before you execute. Sometimes, we can quite harmlessly use the 'Trial and Error' method to solve problems'. My brother and I were fishing once in Florida off a pier and not catching anything. In fact, the crabs were eating all our bait. I tried changing the bait, changing the weight, and moving it around a bit and nothing worked. Finally, I threw the bait out, let it sink, and then raised it up a couple feet and WHAM, a nice, speckled trout. I did the same thing and another and another. I told my brother what to do and we both caught several nice (and tasty) speckled trout. I tried several things before I found a tactic that worked. Life and work are a little more complex than fishing and have bigger issues. After you identify the problem, do some due diligence and explore every possible solution to resolve it. Don't be afraid to ask other managers. They may have been through the

same problem and successfully navigated through it. Their input is what we call, 'best demonstrated practices'. Someone that is doing something well or has resolved an issue offers to share the solution to others with similar issues. This is a definite plug for networking with other managers. We should always be in the learning mode and never too proud to ask for assistance.

4.   Follow up soon and frequently to ensure the solution resolved this issue. If it does, continue and tweak as needed. If it doesn't, go back to the planning stage and develop another plan.

I like to put issues or problems into three categories. Those that I can control, those that I can contribute to the solution, and those that I can't do either. Some things are above us and we have no control over them. Some things, we can add our small part to the solution. Then, there are those that we can determine the outcome by presenting a viable solution.

I am adding this because it is very important that you be very transparent with your team as to your level of involvement. If it is out of your hands, they need to know that. If you are in control, then they also need to know that and help you develop a solution. Your staff thinks your section needs another employee. You request the additional hire through corporate but are denied (Out of your control). You tell the team that you requested the extra person, but it was denied. They at least they know you tried. Then, you use the problem-solving technique above because you bought this great book. You know that staffing is calculated by production numbers, so you get with your team and say, "I have an idea" (Some contribution).

You all work hard to find ways to produce the numbers required to hire an additional person. Once you reach that number, corporate tells you that it is your call as to whether or not you hire someone. The caveat is that you are expected to keep production up and stay within your budget. (More on finances later. Bet you can't wait for that chapter.) Now you (totally in control) deliver the news and the expectations to the team, everyone loves you and yes, yet another happy ending.

One last thing on problems. You can BEST handle problems when you are at your BEST (You say, 'Wow, this guy is deep'. Ha Ha I denote a tad bit of sarcasm there). You should always be operating at your best, but you especially have to be at your best when problems arise. I have been making comments all through this book on reading and learning and growing as a leader. This has been called, 'Sharpening your saw'. Getting and staying sharp is well worth all the time and effort you put into it.

It's spring and time for the first yard work. The blades on the lawn mowers are a bit dull as are the pruning shears and the weed eater needs a new sparkplug. You head out anyhow to start. You have to start the weed eater over and over again and then it finally stops. You have so much trouble with the hedges because of the dull shears and the grass looks terrible. Preparation is one step you do not want to skip. It will take you so much more time and effort in everyday operations and problem solving if you are not sharp.

I have a bookshelf, full of good books on leadership and management. I also have several notebooks with notes I have taken from the books and also past experiences that I have gleaned helpful processes from. I review those notes often and have them pretty well categorized so that I can get to the right subject quickly.

My tools of choice are a three-ring notebook and a 3-hole punch. I can write notes on notebook paper but also print things off I find of interest and insert them into my notes. I also create tabs (using the dividers you can buy with the little plastic topic holders) for the various subjects (You can order a copy of my notebook for four easy installments of Order now and get a free pen). You know whose notebook will be the best? Yours! Because it will be a living notebook that you add to and review frequently. (All this tremendous organizational advice is actually included in this book at no extra cost)

CHAPTER 8

FINANCES

If you are a manger and do not have to deal with finances, jump for joy—but, I would imagine most of you do. Besides personnel issues, finances are probably the most unpleasant things you have to deal with. I have often said this, "You as the manager, have the responsibility of producing the most and the best products or services, maintain a great team through workplace satisfaction, all within the confines of a tiny budget." That is what makes management one of the hardest roles one can get into. Just a few things about finances.

1. Every For-profit business has to produce a profit in order to continue operations. No matter how much you focus on quality and employee satisfaction, you will go under if you are not profitable. Profit very simply put is your revenue minus your expenses. **REVENUE – EXPENSES = PROFIT**. So, you take the revenue you get in from your products and services and subtract the expenses you incurred while supplying them and that will result in your profit.

2. Remember the BIG PICTURE. Your section has a budget but as you go up the ladder, those above you all have bigger budgets until you come to the company

wide budget. So, looking at both points, it is your role to increase your revenue and decrease your expenses, so that your area of oversight will meet budget. If all the sections meet budget, the company will as well.

3. Your role, INCREASING REVENUE, DECREASING EXPENSES, can be divided into two categories. The things you can control and the things you can't control. You can't make people buy your services or products, but you can help control customer satisfaction which will in turn increase revenue. You can't control the rent, taxes, or the utilities, but you can control supply costs and labor costs. 'I can't control what my employees make. They have set salaries.' Yes, they do but you can control productivity which in ensuring that the hours worked correlate with the products or services provided. You can also help control overtime which is one of the key drivers of high labor costs. You can only do so much, but you better be doing all that you can do. Just one example here, although I could give so many. I had a section once that had horrible labor numbers causing us to be over budget. I started being the first one in and the last one to leave. I wanted to picture everything that was going on. Here are just a few things that I noticed.

A. Although not everyone's areas started first thing in the morning, they all came in at the same time.

B. Although some got finished in their areas earlier in the day, they stayed until everyone left. Now, putting these two together, consider this; Nonproductive hours always affect your productivity. If it is a lag time in the middle of the day, not much can be done. But, at the beginning and the end of the day, there is usually a way to cut down on these hours especially because some become overtime hours.

C. A couple of people were staying after all the work was done to do "additional tasks". This again increased hours, and some were overtime.

D. I also noticed that there was plenty of slow time during the day to get those additional tasks done.

PAUSE: I need to add something before I go on to share my action plan. Finances are everyone's responsibility, although the manager will focus on it a great deal more that the staff. Managers need to be very clear on their role on managing finances and how the team can help. One way to help is to be receptive when the manager makes adjustments to help with productivity and labor costs. Your manager wants you working just as hard on that as your team does at their assigned tasks. Make sure your team understands that and ask for their buy in.

My action plan was quite simple. Each employee was given a time specific schedule. Instead of D for dayshift, it now said 7:30 AM or 8:00 AM depending on their tasks. The end time was the same. No one was to clock in more than 10 minutes before their starting time without prior permission and everyone had to clock out when they were finished. I also divided up the additional tasks among all of them so they could be completed during the down time. As far as labor goes, we were back in the green in no time.

4. Remember, a lot of little bits added up, make a lot. I was a Director in the Tidewater Virginia area for a dialysis company. One of my clinics was way over on their supply budget. I visited the clinic and looked around a bit. It wasn't long before I saw something that made my financial Spidey sense alert. One of the technicians was taking a patient off of the machine. She had a pack that was made up earlier in the day. That pack, (I counted them) and a wad of 10 gauze sponges. It usually took about 4-5 to take a patient off and get them going. I then noticed that all the packs were like that. When the techs made the packs up, they just threw in a handful of these gauze sponges. Some may have had more than 10, others a couple less but it averaged around 10. So, let's say they were throwing away 5 sponges per patient. The patients dialyze three times a week so that is 15 gauze sponges per week. The company has 200,000 patients so if all the clinics wasted 5 sponges per patient per treatment,

that would equal 3 million gauze sponges a week, **thrown away**. Think that might have an impact on the company's budget? In the other example I gave of the extra hours, we decreased roughly 10.5 hours of overtime a week. Overtime is time and a half. Let's just say the average salary was $20 an hour. So, the 10.5 X $10 (overtime addition) = $105 a week x 52 weeks = $5460 a year. Little adds up to big. I think you get the point.

A Note on Micromanagement

This statement may make you say. 'Ah phooey (is that actually a word?)'. 'He doesn't know what he is talking about.' Please keep reading and I think you will have to agree. **Everything needs to be micromanaged**. Now, I did not say that EVERYONE needs to be micromanaged, but everything does. Micromanagement basically means getting down to the smallest unit to see if things are functioning properly. To make sure that things have the best quality and are as efficient as they can be, they have to be micromanaged. But let me say this as well, if the things aren't being micromanaged properly, then the micromanagement will have to carry over to responsible individuals.

Let's use our supply cost in another example. While reviewing the Regional financials, the Regional Vice President notices that the supply cost is over budget. He looks to see which areas are over budget and sends a message to the Directors of those areas to identify the causes of the overage. That is management. The Directors, in turn, look to see which sections are over and sends those managers a message to look for causes. That is management. The managers then go to their supply persons and ask why the section was over in supply costs. That is management. The supply person then digs into the ordering, the inventory, stock on hand and checks the files for any unusual purchases. That is MICROMANAGEMENT. They are doing their job to identify the root causes that we discussed earlier.

Now, a week goes by and the manager hasn't heard from the supply person. That person may also need some micromanagement and so forth up the chain. Best case scenario is to have all the micromanagement done at the lowest possible level. Managers, Directors and above should not ever have to be micromanaged. It does happen, however usually, with a not so happy ending. As a manger, everyone is your section that has a responsibility should micromanage it so that no person has to be micromanaged.

Your labor cost is high, did you dive in to find out why? Do that deep dive we talked about. The products are not selling, the business is not flourishing, the harvest is smaller, and the cars don't run as well. Whatever the problem is, dig deep and micromanage every **aspect** so that **you** won't have to be micromanaged (By the way, your boss is doing the same thing, and their boss, and their boss. I think you got this).

One more important note on micromanagement: **Do not micromanage *people* that are doing a good job micromanaging their *area of responsibility*.** It may seem to you like you are adding an extra layer of micromanagement, but you are diminishing the appearance of trust and respect that you have for them. This deteriorates the relationship that you have been working so hard to create. Empower them, trust them and routinely monitor, (not micromanage) their processes and products.

CHAPTER 9

TEAMWORK

We have talked some about this throughout the previous chapters, but I want to make some specific comments about it here. We cannot say enough about teamwork. More can be accomplished as a team than all the individual efforts combined. Everyone leaning on the strengths and fortifying the weakness of others enables teamwork to achieve great results.

Some people are very good at what they do but they are not so good at working together with others as a team. They probably got a 'Doesn't play well with others' remark on their report card in first grade. The manager's responsibility isn't just to get everyone to do their job well, but also combine their efforts with others to improve the overall outcome.

I can see how the military worked to instill the value of teamwork in new recruits as they entered basic training. I remember learning how to march, for example. Everyone starts out on the same foot and the cadence is called out so that everyone in marching at the same pace. When we would go to the dining hall, there were tables of four set up and no one could sit down until there were recruits standing at all four chairs. Then, we all sat down at the same time.

Sometimes, they would offer incentives (like an extra hour of free time during the day) for stellar performances, such as a demerit free uniform inspection. The key was that either everyone would get the incentive, or no one would. So, if one person did not pass, no one got the incentive. You should have seen us all going around and inspecting each other. That's teamwork. Teamwork is crucial in the military as it could save many lives during a battle.

It is just as important in your workplace although hopefully, no one will get shot at as they work. Teaching people how to work is one thing, teaching them how to work together as a team is quite another. Some of the key words involved is trust, communication, reliance, and cooperation. All of these have to be present for teamwork to operate effectively.

We need to remember that everyone on the team has to contribute even though everyone's contributions may be different. Let's look at yet another ingenious illustration (I have tons of them). A tug of war match is going on. There are three average men on one side and one NFL lineman on the other side. The first match is just barely won by the three men. The player calls me over and asks me to help (I was wearing a muscle shirt, so he was probably impressed with all my rippled muscles—not to mention that I was the only one there). Anyhow, I joined the match and we won. Now, the questions. 1) Was my contribution needed for success? The answer is, yes. 2) Did I contribute as much as the NFL player? Not hardly.

What if I was on his team but offered no contribution; then, we would have lost. Even though my contribution was much less, it put us over the line. (Actually, we pulled them over the line. Tug of war, remember?)

I was taking night classes at a nearby university. I was getting all A's until I got to Biology. We had 'group' projects and my group's project was to party and let me do all the work. I finally had to depend on them to come up with a few things for a project and well, I got my first ever B in college. (I only got one B in high school too, but the other grades were not A's) [frowney face].

What I am saying, and what everyone needs to understand is that in order to win, everyone needs to contribute even though everyone's contributions will not be the same. This is critical to understands in workplaces where people have different roles. There are hierarchies in some workplaces. For example, in the dialysis clinics there are technicians, nurses, charge nurses, a manager, secretaries, biomedical people and others. Some have what are seemingly more important roles or perhaps advanced would be a better word. But, believe me—everyone is important and it is your role as a manager to make sure everyone feels that way. The nurses may carry the heavy patient responsibilities, but if our admin didn't do their part; we would be lost.

I remember that shortly after I became a nurse, I was at work and all my assignments were caught up. I started helping the technicians with some of the stuff they had to do, and the charge nurse yelled out, "Hey Allen, you are a nurse now. You don't have to do that anymore." Well, you should have seen the looks he got from the technicians that I was helping. Was it my job to do it? Yes, it was. It wasn't an assigned task, but contributed to the overall mission of the team (That nurse was not voted 'most liked person' on that team.

One habit I had was when I need a special project done, I would assign two or three people to accomplish it. Now, it might only need one person but creating a team to do the project got them to work together collaboratively.

Picture this at a car dealership. The front of the lot was divided into three sections. There are three workers responsible for ensuring their section of cars are neat and clean. Another way to do this would be to tell the three workers that they don't have sections anymore, but the three of them are responsible for all the cars on the front of the lot. You will probably see them discussing a plan; one will probably rise to take a bit of leadership and they will communicate so much more during the workday.

The original plan needed no communication, trust, or reliance. The second one did and at the end of the day, the three were able to say, "WE did it." (Then, they all went out and celebrated together and we have yet another wonderfully happy ending).

It is also to get into a habit of using the words 'we' and 'our' as opposed to 'me' and 'my' as much as possible. Make sure you attribute your successes and accomplishments to the efforts the team.

I have been debating on whether or not to put this in, but I feel it so likely illustrates the point here. (You will see why I hesitated in a minute.) The body had a meeting one day to choose what parts would be considered the MVP (Most Valuable Parts) of the body.

The heart said, "Well, of course I am in. If it wasn't for me, you would all die because you wouldn't get any blood."

The lungs responded, "And they need that blood because it has oxygen in it because I put it there, so I am in."

The brain answered, "Well, if I didn't signal you all to do what you do, it wouldn't get done, so I am in."

Then everyone heard a meek voice. It was the rectum. "What about me?" Everyone busted out laughing. What an absurd thought. It wanted to be recognized with the brain and the heart and the lungs? The rectum said, "Fine, I quit."

A week later the rectum was voted in as one of the MVPs.

I will wait till you are done laughing to continue. The point is, everyone is important when we are talking about the team. The general, yes sir. The private, you bet—as well as everyone in between.

I want to mention one more thing. You are a part of the team in your workplace. What other teams are you a part of? In my world, several managers were a team under a director. We got together for meetings and were on calls together. Be a good team player with your other teams as well. This is where you have access to so much in the line of networking.

Some managers excel at some things and others do well in other things. As a part of this team, you have access to processes and ideas that can help your workplace team. Don't be afraid to contribute during the meetings either because I am sure you have some things that would be beneficial to others as well. I have heard so many people that have said that they just want to work by themselves. They have obviously not tapped into the wonderful world of team.

CHAPTER 10

DELEGATION

Oh my, we are on the last chapter. Time sure flies unless you have been reading this book over a long period of time. Personally, I think it is one of those, 'I can't put it down', books. I know you are saying you had no trouble putting it down. Thanks, I already have a self-esteem issue. You say, 'Sure, doesn't seem like it.' If you quit talking back, we can move on.

The last subject we are going to look at is delegation. This is a very important subject. In order for you to be successful and create additional capacity, you need to be able to delegate. I cannot talk about delegation without emphasizing this phrase, 'shared accountability'. That basically means that you are sharing (not relinquishing) the accountability of the delegated task with another. You are ultimately still accountable, but have shared that accountability with another person. Delegating responsibility is a great way to help your employees grow and it also gives them a sense of empowerment. It increases the fulfillment they have in their job, creating a little more motivation. Let's go through the process.

1.   Make sure you pick the right person for the job. In the first dialysis clinic that I managed, (the one we discussed earlier), once I got all new staff in, it was

several months before I delegated anything. I wanted to learn about the strengths of everyone on the team so that I knew what they excelled in. Some showed some leadership traits, others were good at clerical tasks, some very matriculate and thorough. When I needed to delegate something, I could choose the right person. NOTE: Never delegate something just to get some help and create more capacity for yourself. If you do not have a solid candidate for the task, develop someone and in the meantime, keep doing it yourself. Believe me, it is not worth it, and you will actually create more time-consuming problems.

2. The initial discussion is also very important. You should never start out with, 'I have a job for you,' or 'I want to make you my inventory specialist.' The best way to start the discussion is something like this, "Joey, I am looking for someone to oversee inventory and I thought of you. Would you be open to discussing this?" Wow, you thought of him. That starts the conversation off on a positive note, yet you have not asked him to take the role, just wondered if he would be open to discussing it. That gives Joey an opportunity to bow out without any pressure very gracefully. If Joey is interested, then you can proceed with what the role entails, any underlying issues, what the expectations are, what the end result should look like and what additional training they will need to complete. In this case, for example:

Underlying Issue: The team runs out of some supplies while there are stockpiles of others. There is no process for supply management. The need is for someone to adequately manage inventory and supplies.

What does the role entail?: The role entails establishing a process for proficiently managing supplies. Par levels should be set for items and extra inventory should be considered before future ordering.

The Expectations: It will be expected that a process will be developed, monitored, and tweaked as needed, to ensure accurate inventory counts and enhance the ordering system.

The End Result: The process should ensure that the workplace never runs out of supplies and never develops a stockpile of extra supplies.

Training Required: There are a few computer based courses that you would need to take in order to fully understand the inventory process and ordering system. We would then have you work with an experienced inventory specialist for a day to ensure you are confident to handle the task. And of course, I am always available to help you.

I would always end the conversation asking for questions and telling them if they needed some time to think about it, that would be fine.

3. The training is vital, should be thorough and should not be rushed. You want to make sure they are not set up to fail by giving them a responsibility and not giving the training and time they need to become competent. I have been given additional roles and the training went like this, 'Here is a book with everything you need to know and even some examples. If you have any questions you can call the guy at _____ and he can help. Thanks so much for taking this on.' Now, if I hadn't been a self-starting, motivated, outgoing, and ambitious person, I would have failed miserably. Start the training off correctly, monitor it frequently, and BE PATIENT. I have frequent check-ins during the training, giving them a chance to ask questions and also to assess if they are progressing and still bought in to the role. When I delegated something that I had personally been doing, I would often go through a series of steps with them to ensure were on the same page.

A. Step 1: I would do the task and have them observe.
B. Step 2: I would do the task and ask for them to contribute.
C. Step 3: I would work with them to do the task.

D. Step 4: I would have them do the task, with me present for any assistance they may need.
E. Step 5: I would have them do it alone and then check everything over with them.

We call this 'On the job training'. People can learn so much by seeing, and so much by hearing; but add doing, and the learning increases tremendously.

4. After the task has been delegated, the monitoring stage begins. When does this end? NEVER. It can decrescendo (I had to get at least one big word in this book), and the intervals and intensity may be lowered. Remember, delegation is shared accountability, not relinquished. You, as the manager, are still ultimately responsible for the outcome.

NOTE: I want to share one more thing with you on this shared accountability. I have heard so many managers blame unsatisfactory outcomes on a person that they had delegated a task. That is a very poor trait for a manger to have. The buck stops here. Don't blame someone else to keep yourself out of hot water. If you were monitoring it as you should have, the results could have been different. Should that employee ever find out you did that, you just lost any respect you may have garnered.

Delegation is a wonderful tool in your toolbox. When used properly, it can aid you tremendously and create more capacity for you to be able to do other things. I have often said that we want to hire managers with creative, out of the box thinking capabilities, but then we don't give them time to do it. Delegation can help!

CONCLUSION

Management is a wonderful role to get into if you are a true leader, if you are willing to further develop your leadership skills, and you have the right 'WHY' for being a leader. If I have had any success in my role as a leader, it has been because I understand that leaders lead people, not just things.

By the way, I do not measure my success as a leader by how many things I have done, but by how many people I have touched in some way or another. That is why I am writing this book. I hope it has helped. I wish you all the success in the world.

Allen Daugherty

Printed in the United States
By Bookmasters